To read fluently is one of the basic aims of anyone learning English as a foreign language. **And it's never too early to start**. Ladybird Graded Readers are interesting but simple stories designed to encourage children between the ages of 6 and 12 to read with pleasure.

Reading is an excellent way of reinforcing language already acquired, as well as broadening a child's vocabulary. Ladybird Graded Readers use a limited number of grammatical structures and a carefully controlled vocabulary, but where the story demands it, a small number of words outside the basic vocabulary are introduced. In **_Cinderella_** the following words are outside the basic vocabulary for this grade:

ball _(dance)_**, cinders, coach, coachman, coal, diamond, fairy godmother, footman, lizard, mouse, mousetrap, pumpkin, rat, rat trap, strike, ugly, wand, wave**

Further details of the structures and vocabulary used at each grade can be found in the Ladybird Graded Readers _leaflet._

British Library Cataloguing in Publication Data

Ullstein, Sue
   Cinderella.
   1. English language—Readers
  I. Title   II. Price Thomas, Brian
  III. Perrault, Charles, _1628-1703_. Cendrillon
  428.6
  ISBN 0-7214-1349-9

First edition

Published by Ladybird Books Ltd Loughborough Leicestershire UK
Ladybird Books Inc Auburn Maine 04210 USA

Printed in England

Cinderella

retold by Sue Ullstein
illustrated by Brian Price Thomas

Ladybird Books

This is the story of a young girl called Cinderella. She has a hard life. Her mother is dead, and she lives with her father and her two older sisters. Cinderella's sisters do not like her because she is very beautiful. They are jealous of her. Their own faces are ugly because they are always angry. They are often unkind to Cinderella.

The ugly sisters make Cinderella do all the housework. She has to carry the coal for the fire. She has to cook the meals and wash the dishes. She has to wash all the clothes. She works from morning till night.

Cinderella also has to help her sisters with their clothes. She cleans their shoes. She brushes and combs their hair. She does *everything* for them!

The two older sisters have a lot of beautiful clothes but they look ugly. Their clothes do not make them beautiful. Cinderella has no beautiful clothes. She has only an old grey dress and old wooden shoes. But she always looks beautiful.

Cinderella does not have a bedroom. She has to sleep in the kitchen. She sleeps in the cinders by the fire. And so her family call her Cinderella.

One day, the king decides to give a big party for his son, the prince. The party will go on for three days, and each evening there will be a great ball. The king invites all the beautiful girls in the country. He wants the prince to choose a wife.

The king invites Cinderella's two ugly sisters but he does not invite Cinderella. He does not know about her because she never goes out. Everyone thinks that she is her sisters' servant.

On the evening of the first ball, Cinderella helps her sisters. They put on their new dresses and Cinderella brushes and combs their hair.

Then Cinderella sits down at the top of the stairs. She watches her sisters.

''I'd like to go to the ball, too,'' she says sadly. She begins to cry.

''Why are you crying?'' the ugly sisters ask angrily.

''I'd like to wear a beautiful dress,'' Cinderella answers. ''I'd like to go to the ball, too.''

''You? Go to the ball?'' the ugly sisters laugh. ''You can't go to the king's ball. You have no beautiful clothes.''

The ugly sisters leave the house and Cinderella goes back to her kitchen. She cries and cries. She is very sad.

Suddenly Cinderella hears a kind voice.

"Why are you crying, my dear?" it says.

Cinderella jumps up. An old lady is standing behind her. She is smiling.

"I'd like to go to the ball," Cinderella replies. "I'd like to wear a beautiful dress and meet the prince."

"You *can* go to the ball," the old lady says.

"But how can I go to the ball?" Cinderella asks.

"I'm your fairy godmother, Cinderella," the old lady says. "I can do magic. Now dry your eyes and listen carefully.

"First, go into the garden and bring me a pumpkin. I need the biggest pumpkin in the garden."

"Yes, of course," Cinderella answers. She runs outside.

She picks a pumpkin and takes it to
her fairy godmother. The fairy
godmother touches the pumpkin with
her magic wand. At once it becomes
a golden coach!

"Now bring me the <u>mousetrap</u> from the kitchen," the fairy godmother says.

"Yes, of course," Cinderella replies. She runs to the kitchen.

Soon she brings back the mousetrap. There are six mice in it.

<u>The fairy godmother touches the mousetrap with her magic wand. The mousetrap opens and the six mice run out.</u>

The fairy godmother touches the mice with her magic wand. At once they become six beautiful grey horses!

"Now bring me the rat trap," the fairy godmother says.

"Yes, of course," Cinderella answers.

Soon she comes back with the rat trap. There is one rat in it.

The fairy godmother touches the rat trap with her magic wand. The rat trap opens and the rat runs out. The fairy godmother touches the rat with her magic wand. At once it becomes a coachman! He will drive Cinderella's coach.

"And lastly, bring me two lizards from the garden," the fairy godmother says.

"Yes, of course," Cinderella replies.

She runs into the garden and finds two small lizards.

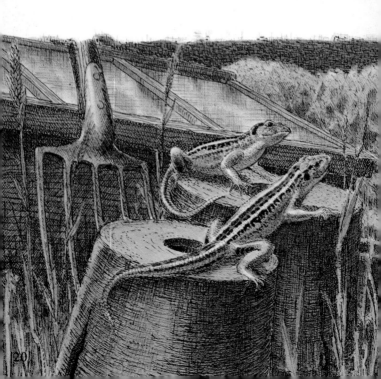

When the fairy godmother touches the lizards with her magic wand, they become two footmen! They go and stand at the back of the coach.

Now Cinderella has a golden coach, six grey horses, a coachman and two footmen.

Sadly she looks down at her old grey dress and her wooden shoes.

"One more touch with my magic wand!" her fairy godmother says. And now the most wonderful magic of all happens!

Cinderella's old grey dress and wooden shoes disappear. Now she is wearing a beautiful pink balldress. There are pink flowers in her hair and pink shoes on her feet.

Cinderella is very happy.
''Oh, thank you, thank you, Fairy
Godmother!'' she cries.

"Have a good time at the ball, my dear," the fairy godmother says. "But remember one thing. You must be home before midnight. After the clock strikes twelve, the coach will become a pumpkin again. The horses will become mice, the coachman will be a rat again and the footmen will be lizards. And your dress will be old and grey again."

"I'll be home by midnight," Cinderella says, "I promise." And she kisses her fairy godmother.

25

When Cinderella arrives at the king's palace, her ugly sisters do not know her. She looks so beautiful! Everyone thinks that she is a princess from another country.

The prince thinks that Cinderella is the most beautiful girl at the ball. He asks her to dance and then he dances with her all evening.

Cinderella has a wonderful time at the ball, but she keeps her promise to her fairy godmother. She leaves the ballroom at a quarter to twelve. The other people are still dancing.

Cinderella's coach is waiting for her. When she arrives home the clock is striking twelve.

As she opens the door, her beautiful pink balldress disappears. The coach becomes a pumpkin again. The horses become mice, the coachman is a rat and the footmen are lizards.

Cinderella goes back to her kitchen. She sits down in the cinders by the fire.

Soon the ugly sisters arrive home. They tell Cinderella about the beautiful princess at the ball.

"The prince danced with her all evening!" they say. "But no one knows anything about her. Who is she?"

Cinderella smiles, but she does not say anything!

The next evening the ugly sisters go to the second ball. They leave Cinderella in the kitchen. She sits in the cinders by the fire. But soon her fairy godmother comes again. She waves her magic wand and the golden coach, the six grey horses, the coachman and the two footmen appear again.

This time Cinderella's balldress is blue and silver. It is more beautiful than the pink dress. She has silver stars in her hair and blue and silver shoes on her feet.

"Oh, thank you, thank you, Fairy Godmother!" Cinderella cries.

"Have a good time at the ball, my dear," the fairy godmother says. "But remember, you must be home by midnight!"

"Yes, I promise," Cinderella says. And she kisses her fairy godmother.

When Cinderella arrives at the
palace the prince comes to her at
once.

"Will you dance with me, please?"
he asks. And again he dances
with Cinderella all
evening.

Everyone watches Cinderella.
"Who's that beautiful girl?" they ask
again and again. But no one knows.

Cinderella has a wonderful time at
the ball. It is five to twelve when she
remembers her promise. She leaves
the ballroom quickly.

when? why?
when does C. leave the ball at
the second ball?
why does C. leave the ballroom quickly
the second evening?

coachma, coachman, footmen, horses, ci

The coach is waiting for her. But they are only half way home when the clock strikes twelve.

The coach and horses, the coachman and the footmen all disappear. *Why*

Cinderella is *Why* alone in the dark street. She is wearing her old grey dress and wooden shoes again.

She has to run home. *Why* She arrives a few minutes before her ugly sisters. They find her in the cinders by the fire in the kitchen.

Again the ugly sisters talk about the beautiful princess at the ball.

''The prince danced with her all evening!'' they say. ''But no one knows her name. Who is she?''

Again Cinderella smiles, but she does not say anything!

why

because she is the princess her self

On the evening of the third ball, Cinderella's fairy godmother comes again. She waves her magic wand, and the golden coach, the six grey horses, the coachman and the two footmen appear again.

This time Cinderella's dress is silver and gold. It is the most beautiful dress of the three.

Tonight she has diamonds in her hair and round her neck. She has golden shoes on her feet.

"Oh, thank you, thank you, Fairy Godmother," she says.

"Have a good time at the ball, my dear," her fairy godmother says. "But remember, you must be home by midnight!"

"Yes, I promise," Cinderella replies. And she kisses her fairy godmother.

When Cinderella arrives at the
palace the prince is waiting for her.

"Please dance with me again," he
asks.

"Yes, of course," Cinderella
answers.

They dance together all evening.
Cinderella has a wonderful time. She
forgets about her promise to her fairy
godmother. Suddenly the clock starts
to strike twelve.

Cinderella runs out of the ballroom,
but she loses one of her golden
shoes! Sadly, the prince picks it up.

"Where has my beautiful princess gone?" he asks. But no one knows.

Cinderella runs to her coach, but it has disappeared. She has to run all the way home. why? because her has disappear

The prince looks everywhere for his princess. He has fallen in love with her. He wants to marry her.

The next morning, the prince takes
the golden shoe to his father and
says, "Father, I want to marry the girl
who owns this shoe. But how can I
find her? I don't know her name."

And so the king sends the prince
and his servants out into the city.
They take the golden shoe and they
visit every girl who went to the ball.

Every girl tries the shoe on. Every
girl hopes that it will fit her, but the
shoe is always too small.

At last the prince comes to
Cinderella's house.

The ugly sisters try on the golden shoe, but it does not fit. Their feet are too big. They cannot marry the prince. They are very angry. *why*

Then the prince asks Cinderella's father, ''Have you any more daughters?''

"I have one more," the father replies. "But she's always in the kitchen. She didn't go to the ball."

"She's too dirty!" the ugly sisters cry. "The shoe won't fit her!"

But the prince says, "Please bring her here. She must try the shoe on, too."

Cinderella comes in. She takes off her old wooden shoe. Then she tries on the golden shoe. It fits! *why? because its hers*

Cinderella stands up. The prince looks at her face. Yes — this is the beautiful girl who danced with him at the ball.

"Will you marry me?" he asks.

Suddenly Cinderella's fairy godmother appears. She waves her magic wand and Cinderella becomes a beautiful princess again. The ugly sisters are very angry and very jealous!

The prince takes Cinderella to his father's palace.

Soon the prince marries Cinderella. Everyone is happy — except the ugly sisters!

And Cinderella and the prince live happily ever after.